LANDING

Also by Warren Woessner:

THE FOREST AND THE TREES, 1968
THE RIVERS RETURN, 1969
INROADS, 1970
CROSS-COUNTRY, 1972

Warren Woessner

LANDING

an Ithaca House book

Ithaca

Many of these poems have appeared in *Abraxas, Connections,* COSMEP Anthology 2, *Cronopios, December, Doones, The Dragonfly, Epoch, Folio, Foxfire, Hanging Loose, Hearse, It, Kumquat, La Huerta, The Nation, The North Stone Review, Poetry Northwest, Quixote, South Dakota Review, Tampa Poetry Review, Upriver* and *Wisconsin Review.*

"Getting The Laundry", "Black Crow", "Operation", "Return From Absolute Zero" and "Laos In The Air" first appeared in *Poetry.*

Copyright 1973 by Ithaca House

ISBN 0-87886-035-5 cloth
ISBN 0-87886-036-3 paper

All rights reserved. No part of this book may be reproduced without written permission of the publisher except for brief excerpts in reviews.

ITHACA HOUSE
108 N. PLAIN STREET
ITHACA, NEW YORK 14850

CONTENTS

Refuge

Getting The Laundry :   3
Eagles :   4
Last Refuge :   5
The Colossal Horned Owl :   6
The Butterflies Return :   7
Graveyard At Cripple Creek, Colorado :   8
Closed Camp :   9
Black Crow :   10
Navajo Poem :   11
Mountains :   12
Precipitation Indices :   13
Adaptation :   14
An Erasure :   15
Six A.M. :   16
Retreat :   17
Silence :   18

Inroads

October :   21
Hunting Agates At Two Harbors :   22
Door :   23
Visions :   24
No Cover For Stag Girls :   25
Winter Solstice :   26
December Fields :   27
Flitcraft's Woods :   28
The Wind :   29
Way To Go :   30
Report From Iowa :   31
Farm Auction :   32
North Country :   33

Storm Over Woodstown : 34
Inlet : 35
Country Graveyard : 36

Landing

Plains Song : 39
Lost Country : 40
The Owl : 41
Operation : 42
After Pain : 43
Return From Absolute Zero : 44
Laos In The Air : 45
Letter To Viet Nam : 46
The Skeleton Crew : 47
Epitaph For Mildred : 48
Retouching : 49
Waiting : 50
Timepiece : 51
Power Failure : 52

REFUGE

GETTING THE LAUNDRY

Rest has come again. The cars
push their echoes,
read the road like braille.
The tired squeak of a single tricycle rolls home.
I look up to see a half-moon not quite included
by the Power Co-op/Truck Service signs.
It has time yet to land safely in the dark.
The last patch of dirt in front of the new GTC
has hardened into asphalt.
Again, there is time.
I find myself folding the laundry
more slowly than I could. It is a simple thing to do.
A thing missed, like picking fruit
or sanding wood. Also the warmth.
Clothes have the patience of old friends:
with open doors, always on my side.

EAGLES

1. Salem, N.J.

A heron probed the shallows
and two pintails casually moved away
but the huge nest we hoped to spot was gone:
left empty then fallen like an old house
when the owners move away or die.

2. Brigantine Wildlife Refuge

Chased by hawks, a single golden eagle
hunted low over the marsh.
Head down, thick shoulders punching the air,
he flew with the black power of a warlock
searching the swamp for lost hunters.

3. Mississippi River

Perched above a tiny pool in the frozen channel,
a bald eagle, large as a silver dollar, stretched
then soared over the empty trees.
Looking up, I wanted to salute, sing,
believe in freedom. For a moment America
was beautiful again.

LAST REFUGE

No, I don't know where I was.
You found me by the trail
with a full canteen six days
after it was empty
and I'd stumbled miles down the mountain
I had tried to climb,
into some cave outside my map.
I dropped, slept, and woke
to birds singing forgotten songs.
I swear an ivory-billed woodpecker
drilled a tree nearby the whole valley
was thick with buffalo and tiny deer.
Flocks of pigeons I'd seen
in pictures somewhere filled the chestnut trees.
I found a clear stream covered with huge swans
and drank and slept again.
You found me where they put me,
easy to find, kidnapped from the land of the dead.

THE COLOSSAL HORNED OWL

Darkness, his eyes
open
start decoding.
Dropping from deep
in the branches:
the deadliest fruit
hunting for throats.
Huge wings snap:
lights go out.
Rats, foxes, babies
left by open windows,
lovers too far
off the path;
all are taken up
in a rush of sharp air.
At daybreak, they are found
digested into perfect balls
of hair, gut,
and bone.
All sizes
spread around a tree
like frozen planets
deserted by a black star.

THE BUTTERFLIES RETURN

Almost no one remembers them
flying toward our town from all directions,
a tidal wave of wings rising slowly from the prairies.
The first reports were merely quaint. A Candystriper
missed a spare when her ball skidded on a butterfly
that suddenly landed on the lane. A butterfly
flew into the mayor's mouth
while he was speaking on DDT.
The incidents increased until they could not be ignored.
Cars stalled when wings covered the radiators
or jammed the butterfly valves. A plane
skidded off the runway
when it hit a pool of them, waiting there,
it seems to us now.
At last, hungry butterflies, in the honey, in the jam,
drifting in the streets like living snow.
We offer them sugar, mounds of flowers.
They are staying.
The sunlight turns golden, then gray.
In the rustling night, our dreams are filled
with chloroform and pins.

GRAVEYARD AT CRIPPLE CREEK, COLORADO

From the hillside we could see the town
empty as a model railroad
after the children get bored.
We climbed the fence and herded grasshoppers up the path.
Headstones hid in the weeds
like shy animals left to stray.
All day we missed the men
who'd moved and left these dead behind.
There was gold over the mountain
but sometimes life ran out suddenly:
paydirt fading into rock.

CLOSED CAMP

The council fire is dead
from many rains.
Woodpeckers work on the totem poles;
the only axes left to cut at trees.
But now the spider webs
are undisturbed, carved names
have new bark scars. On the trails,
moss collects, and sassafras leaves reach out
like young, untouched hands.

BLACK CROW

> "I am the crow — I am the crow — his skin is my body."
>
>   - Chippewa song.

You went out, hoping
to be given a question or a path
up a mountain you had never seen.
Then the future would release
like a bowstring, and sing like arrow-feathers
flying to the deep end of your dreams.
It was the moon of the cracking trees.
The north wind was like a skinning knife.
Even hunger left you.
At last it was the crows
that held to the branches after the leaves,
croaking like grandfathers, demanding attention.
They carried you away, in pieces, like an ear of corn,
and left you with secret wings
and a strange song on your stiff lips.

NAVAJO POEM

The old man
sits
in the blue shade
of the coke machine.
All day,
tourists steal
his picture.
He has seen the gods
evicted
and the empty land
fill up with roads.
He has hocked
his bracelets
for a place
to rest,
and sold his rings
for peace.
Like water
in the sun,
he evaporates.
At last, the moon
lifts him out
into the painted night.
Friends are waiting.
Coyote sings
old songs.
In the cool sand,
snake
writes his name.

MOUNTAINS

More than postcards, scenery,
geochemistry, once you were spirit:
a transubstantiation of rock:
walls to hold the world together.

Climbed and conquered now,
you are our pyramids. Tombs
for Beo-chi 'di' , Nayeinezgani;
the hosts of forgotten gods.

PRECIPITATION INDICES

A big jet screams in
just ahead of the storm. Brother
backs out the Buick
to rinse off the dust. Clinging
to flowers in the garden
hang hundreds of gasping bees.

ADAPTATION

Don't hate me
when I say
I want you
only for a breath
of fresh air.
Dead wood
can melt ice
with the heat
of its rotting.
Even lichen dissolves rock
given time.
I can make do
with very little.

AN ERASURE

I'm sorry I had to
forget you, repression
makes for martyrs
and immortality. Now,
like a drowned girl you rise
again in my thoughts. The wind circles
to get behind me. Waiting on the beach,
I never know which tide
will turn you up, back
on my doorstep at last.

SIX A.M.

Deep in our lairs, like foxes
or deer, resting from the chase:
we pull the covers higher, wrestle
with dreams, darker
than our locked and curtained rooms.
While outside, bright and loud,
tomorrow already has us surrounded.

RETREAT

Things brighten
as my eyes open
in the dark. A breeze
bends the half-grown
pear trees.
A white cat
slips through the blue spruce
searching for nests. It is
the moon.
Alone, I watch
the neighbor's porch light
burn itself out
a million miles away.

SILENCE

The small eyes
of delicate, rare creatures
open around us.
Faucet drip:
············water sound.
You've got a good watch.
Listen to my cigarette burning!
Take some of this with you.
Wrap it carefully.

INROADS

OCTOBER

Suddenly
drive-ins close,
stand like glass flowers
whose petals have driven away.

Boats are pulled up
and turned over
all along the Fox.

The pumpkins have begun their migration.

Following
outside the car window
at dusk
the reflection of your hands
picking over the fields,
trying to save enough
for winter.

HUNTING AGATES AT TWO HARBORS

This far north in September
the beaches are empty. A few crows
pick over the washed-up trash.
On the bay, one line of ducks
wait for ice. Under a log
bright clumps
of hibernating ladybugs.

These stones have had more time
to cool. They are the smoky orange
of the last sunlight
falling on a dying world.

DOOR

Cold wind off Lake Michigan
rattles brown oak leaves
shakes the crow decoy
perching by the empty feeder.
Pop of guns. Glimpse
of one grouse flying
over brown ferns.
At the point, gulls
tear up fish scraps
on the dock.
Light rain. Driving south.

VISIONS

The signs are all
for a hard winter. Don't
say you couldn't see them:
pines heavy with cones,
foraging squirrels everywhere.
How could you throw me out, thin
and hungry? The smell of snow
sharp on the air, summer ghosts
shaking in the trees.

NO COVER FOR STAG GIRLS

At the corner of Avon
and K-Mart, they wait
with the patience of the ugly,
clustered around the bus stop sign
as if it were warm.
Like birds that have forgotten
how to migrate, they face the winter
down. Endless telephone lines refuse
to release one invitation.
"What d'you guys wanta do?"
Surrounded by barbed wire,
the last herd of buffalo dance,
drink,
kill time until closing.

WINTER SOLSTICE

No more than insects
stuck in amber, or fish
trapped in a shrinking pond,
we feel the stiffening, the first
ice crystals growing in our blood.

The pale sun rushes past
like a new nurse
in the terminal ward.

Weathervanes
always pointing north:
our brittle faces, turn, helplessly,
back into the wind.

DECEMBER FIELDS

In the arctic light
the brown land is reduced
to essentials: fences,
bushes, become monumental.
And while the birches,
sycamores, hold a hint
of coming winter — across the fields
come grackles, ripening like black fruit
on all the starving branches.

FLITCRAFT'S WOODS

The last seeds
are eaten. The birds, retreated
to the backyard feeders
or the pines upland. Leaves
fill up the tracks where raccoons
or possums pushed out for food.
Not a sound; ice has found
the last free water, and, too high to hear,
the vulture turning over us
veers off: below, just snow and trees,
and we're still moving.

THE WIND

South of Rockford air waves pound the car
then on straight stretches carry us south again.
On both sides, wind sweeps the fields clean:
dust and tattered corn leaves swarm across the road
like locusts. Outside a housing development
paper stuck on a chain fence makes a trash collage.
If we forget, the wind reminds us:
this land is a pool table, we are not safe
outside our pockets.
I fight the wheel and remember the story
of the man and his windwagon
blown away and lost across the prairie.

WAY TO GO

At night it is a joy to drive
toward home not too far away.
The telephone poles are lost
in thought. There is room to breathe.
The farmyards sleep like dogs
under the barn lights.
Winnebago ghosts light slow fires
in cornhusk tepees.
A roadsign points the way to Eldorado
but no one turns. Two white tractor tires
mark a drive way outside Rosendale
then the blue reflectors grow and fade.
The lone radio station demands a decision
for Jesus, but I am safe, buried
in the hearts of the saved.

REPORT FROM IOWA

Here the sky leans down and grinds the earth
like a wet sheet of sandpaper
pushed by an insane geologist
trying to erase his mistakes.
The people fight for cover:
so few trees or caves.
Turn over any leaf
and find whole families hiding there.
They secure themselves with private rituals:
festivals, dances, and hymns.
It is said that ancestor worship is still practiced.
Some men have been seen touching
and speaking to dirt
like defeated football coaches,
imagining ancient games,
trying to pick the winning side.

FARM AUCTION

The big house is empty, picked
to the bone, like carrion left
for hawks and vultures. On the lawn,
bed frames, ice skates, empty mason jars;
the guts of life spread out for sale, for
"Who'll give two dolla's, two, two dolla's,
awright one fifty one fifty
one...?"

NORTH COUNTRY

Out in the dark water
feeding trout ripple the lake
like rain. Forgotten logs
split and bleach like bones
between the rocks. Far away,
a diesel loco moans—
like a man who knows his work
is never done.

STORM OVER WOODSTOWN

When the clouds hurry
toward some destination,
and the insects ring out
worriedly, the farm men
sit up on their porches
to keep the lightning company
and hear the big drops
rattle through the corn.

INLET

Water breaking light
facets
on wind-turned stones.

Like millipedes,
piers crawl over
the mud-flats

to yachts, white birds
nested for sleep.

While on the air,
sea gulls rise
like rice-paper kites, low
sun glowing
through thin wings.

Back in the high grass, an egret blossoms
and stumbles into flight.

COUNTRY GRAVEYARD

I would touch you.
I would warm the marble
with your back
in this quiet place
among the rusty stars
and faded flags:
a different celebration
for our ancestors.

LANDING

PLAINS SONG

The wet soil swells,
rises like a loaf
of black bread. Growing
is a new smell in the air.

Slowly, like an old man
with rusty joints,
the windmill begins to turn.

Low clouds follow
the harrows across the fields.
The earth's sweat
is dust.

LOST COUNTRY

Walking, I begin to notice
how the grass survives
between the houses,
how old the trees are.
The shape of the earth appears.
The hill still slopes down to the lake
despite the houses, poles, wires, roads.
I see how it was
after the glacier melted,
how the stones settled down.
One good look
and all our work is gone.

Once I found a deserted street
buried in the woods, broken
by roots.
Virginia creeper and wild onion
pushed out from the cracks.
Branches met down the middle
of "Capitol Avenue."
It was good to see.
If we leave our footsteps
they don't have a chance.

THE OWL

When we'd run down
through the backyards
jumping the creek and playing war
we'd stay away from odd Mrs. Shay
who lived in the big house with a fence
and was a witch.

From the kitchen she could shoot
a look loud as a shotgun
that always scared us off.
I know now she wasn't crazy,
only rich.

Trying to walk quietly
through the stubble at the wood's edge
looking for an owl,
I think of her again, patient,
waiting for our attack,
the companion of our awe, our flight.

OPERATION

I have been released,
certified to walk the streets,
to work, no longer a hurt animal:
shot full of sleep, fit only for hiding.

But the holes where they took blood
are only half-filled, and the long scar
where they took out more still smiles on my neck.

I face my body like an old friend I never wrote
until I needed him, or like a small country
occupied by an army I invited, but could never trust.

AFTER PAIN

The ceiling of my room opens
like an observatory window.
My bed rises into the sky.
At each corner there is the angel
of a successful chemist. Stars
rest on my back like cool hands.
The fingers tremble for musical
instruments. Cool pebbles wash
into my mouth.

RETURN FROM ABSOLUTE ZERO

The anesthetic releases
its patient slowly
the old pain returns.
The shaking fingers
of X-Rays break
and enter. In the dark,
electrons chatter like teeth.
Nerves spark again. Blood
pushes its ice through tubes
cracked like old hose.
The crystal rooms
lose their perfect corners,
close into bubbles.
Energy relaxes, sighing
like a businessman after three drinks.
Crawling out to share our breath,
you crack your shell,
burst into flame.

LAOS IN THE AIR

The second front is sweeping
down on us. Another summer storm
we hear. The air thickens.
On the ground, lights brighten
like frightened eyes, then the wind
crawls through the grass on its belly.
From the west, fire sirens approach.
Wives take radios to the cellar.
In school, their children kneel
under desks. The old storm riders roar down:
the lies, the contradictions, the deadly
understatement. No one says remember: the men gone,
the women coming up into empty houses,
and the storm there still, waiting,
for the children.

LETTER TO VIET NAM

        For Bob

Since you wrote, nothing
happens here. I click
my pen-point in and out.
What
can I show you that you can't see? —
Snow that is water
not ash, leaves
that fall on their own,
things that take care of themselves
without us.

THE SKELETON CREW

Friday night when the 4 to 12 quits the plant
carrying empty lunch pails and dirty clothes
home to wives, heads full of lawns, guns,
and waterskis, the skeleton crew takes over.
Someone has to keep it going: check the gauges,
watch the stirring, keep the stills alive,
draw the endless overtime.
Outside, men screw, sleep, dream—
the factory keeps working, watched over by its own.
Some rise where they went down: out of buildings
that once collapsed like lungs, from cut-rate reactions
that blew and the sudden gasses that burned:
all children of safety programs born too late.
Others have names like lead, cadmium, or mercury,
the forgotten guinea pigs of perfect experiments
with unpublishable results.
Almost visible in the inorganic haze
the coldest ghosts still walk,
putting in their time, waiting for the next shift.

EPITAPH FOR MILDRED

Huge stacks
of kitchen
and bathroom floors
have scattered
like layers of dead skin.
You are off
your knees.

It is in the flowers,
the well-worn.
Chicory and dandelion
stand by the road
like tired servants
waiting for a ride home.

RETOUCHING

Rain slows. Sounds
like coins dropping
into a tin cup
surround us.
Brown pine needles
stick to my feet.
Drinking from the heavy leaves,
the chill of old fears
runs down my throat.
Lightning!
My heart stops, waiting.

WAITING

Coming or going, you don't
notice them — afraid to move,
staying in one place,
like lost hunters, hoping to be found.
They light cigarettes, turn
pages, strike up conversations
with strangers. Only their eyes
betray them — starting up at footsteps
that might be familiar.

TIMEPIECE

I am forgetting
the names of stars
and the places
where I once was many times.
Driving fast, at night,
the white line pulls you right and
left, while the black scroll of the road
keeps winding up behind —
catching cars you pass, signs, windows,
places you never will get back to:
last week, last year, and tomorrow
is always there, arriving: lights
snapping on in dark rooms.

POWER FAILURE

After midnight, I turn the car up our block
and it is as if I've driven over a pass
and onto a vast desert.
The street stretches out dark and quiet.
The signs are all out.
The windows reflect my lights.
Only the snow is moving. It is very bright.
I drive around to see how far the black-out reaches,
turn on the radio to get the news.
A single car passes, and its headlights are the eyes
of a huge fish feeling its way through an ocean canyon.
Then I hear the power is off because a boy
who wanted to die climbed a fence
and threw himself onto the coils
of the Olin substation transformer.
The police report says his body was burning
like a small bonfire of trash.
Suddenly the music comes back on.
I turn the volume up but it keeps fading,
like the last messages from a spaceship,
out of fuel, drifting, beyond rescue.